Without Breaking His Spirit

Taffi L. Dollar

How to Train Up a Child Without Breaking His Spirit
ISBN 1-885072-19-8
Copyright © 1999 by Taffi L. Dollar

Published by:
Creflo Dollar Ministries
P.O. Box 490124
College Park, Georgia 30349

Printed in the United States of America.

TABLE OF CONTENTS

Introduction 4

Ingredients for Good Parenting 6

Train Them Up 10

A Reflection of the Word 21

Defining the Boundaries 24

Conclusion 28

INTRODUCTION

There are two ways to raise a child: the right way or the wrong way—God's way or the world's way. As a parent, you can put your trust in a professional who has limited, clinical knowledge, or you can trust Almighty God, Who, in His infinite wisdom, gave us His Word to properly direct and guide our children.

Psychologists suggest that you reason with your child when he misbehaves. This style of parenting seems to be right for many people. The Bible says, however, that there is a way that seems right to man, but the end of it leads to destruction (Proverbs 16:25).

The Word of God is your manual for living. It gives step-by-step instructions in family matters and is the final authority for living according to God's will. Since the family is a spiritual unit, God's Word must be the final authority for families that choose to live and operate in the will of God. When you train your child according to the Word of God, his success is guaranteed.

Effective parenting is based on the Word of God. Apart from it, you cannot be a good parent, and apart from God, your children will not have the proper direction. If you want your children to grow up to be godly, responsible, loving adults, make sure you train them God's way. *"Train up a child in the way he should go: and when he is old, he will not depart from it"* (Proverbs 22:6).

INGREDIENTS FOR GOOD PARENTING

It is important to understand God's way of shaping a child's will without breaking his or her spirit. The Word of God, particularly the book of Proverbs, gives instructions on teaching and training children. In addition, it provides insight into developing perception toward the things that concern them. It also contains information on how to impart your faith, which is the greatest inheritance you can leave your children.

Perception, or awareness, is a key ingredient to good parenting. You must be able to see what God has placed in your hands through the avenue of your children. The Shunammite woman in 2 Kings was a great woman because she correctly discerned that Elisha was a man of God. It was her awareness of his anointing that enabled her to receive a blessing.

2 Kings 4:8–11

And it fell on a day, that Elisha passed to Shunem, where was a great woman; and she constrained him to eat bread. And so it was, that as oft as he passed by, he turned in thither to eat bread. And she said unto her husband, Behold now, I perceive that this is an holy man of God, which passeth by us continually. Let us make a little chamber, I pray thee, on a wall; and let us set for him there a bed, and a table, and a stool, and a candlestick: and it shall be, when he cometh to us, that he shall turn in thither. And it fell on a day, that he came thither, and he turned into the chamber, and lay there.

The Shunammite woman was aware of the anointing on Elisha's life, although she had never seen or heard of him before. She prepared a room for him to stay in whenever he passed through Shunem. As a result, Elisha blessed her, and no longer barren, one year later, she bore a son. When the boy died, she went to Elisha, who healed him (2 Kings 4:16-37).

Realize that your children have not been given to you by chance. God has not sent them to irritate you or get on your nerves. The Bible says, *"Lo, children are an heritage of the Lord: and the fruit of the womb is his reward"* (Psalm 127:3). God has a purpose for your children. For that reason, perceive them as blessings and begin to see the potential within them. You must understand who they are in His sight. Therefore, no matter how they act in the natural, you will not be distracted from seeing their divine purpose.

God sees your children as signs and wonders in the earth. *"Behold, I and the children whom the Lord hath given me are for signs and for wonders in Israel from the Lord of Hosts, which dwelleth in mount Zion"* (Isaiah 8:18). He sees their end from the beginning. However, many times parents fail to see the big picture. God knows what He has called your children to do. He knows the anointing and the gifts He has placed in them. It's your responsibility to shape their will without breaking their spirit so they can ultimately fulfill God's plan for their lives.

I personally want methods that are going to work. I don't want to embrace the opinion of a child psychologist. I can't rely on his opinion to raise my children because his way is not God's way. Man's ways are not guaranteed to bring the God-kind of results I need. There are too many variables and nothing concrete on which to base man-made theories. I want to know that when I follow the advice I've been given, everything will turn out all right. God's way is perfect—it is the only way for me to get the best results. *"As for God, his way is perfect; the Word of the Lord is tried: he is a buckler to all them that trust in him"* (2 Samuel 22:31).

Therefore, if I follow God's instructions, I can expect His promises to come to pass in my life and in the lives of my children.

TRAIN THEM UP

God's Word has proven itself throughout countless situations in my life. I know the things in this world are temporal. Heaven and earth will pass away, but God's Word will stand forever (Isaiah 40:8). His way is not a passing fad that will be forgotten ten years from now. God's way will outlast all the others.

Since God created the family, He should be the authority in every home. If God is not the final authority and issues are not resolved according to His Word, each person will begin to assume his or her own authority. Remember, your will may not be the will of God. You must allow God and His Word to be Lord over your home.

Your obedience to God's Word will affect how your children operate in this world. Your lifestyle is a reflection of your beliefs and your children will imitate, emulate, and mirror your ways—good or bad. God has a call, a mission, and a purpose for your children, and it is your responsibility to direct them. *"O that there were such an heart in them, that they would fear me, and keep all my commandments always, that it might be well with them, and with their children for ever!"* (Deuteronomy

5:29). Your child's peace, joy, and well-being will be based on whether you obey God's commandments.

Deuteronomy 12:28

Observe and hear all these words which I command thee, that it may go well with thee, and with thy children after thee for ever, when thou doest that which is good and right in the sight of the Lord thy God.

It is vitally important to closely adhere to the instructions in God's manual. Things will not be right if you follow your own opinion concerning child-rearing. As a parent, you must be willing to receive guidance from God. When you follow His instructions, it tells Him that you are teachable, obedient, and trustworthy. God used Abraham because He knew He could trust him.

Genesis 18:18,19

Seeing that Abraham shall surely become a great and mighty nation, and all the nations of the earth shall be blessed in him? For I know him, that he will command his children and his household after him, and they shall keep the way of the Lord, to do justice and judgment; that the Lord may bring upon Abraham that which he hath spoken of him.

Can God trust you as He did Abraham? Can He trust you to instruct your children to follow Him so that He can bring His promises to pass in their lives?

God desires that you train your children in His way so that He can use them to minister to you and others. He wants you to benefit from the Word and from the anointing in your child's life. That's why in our church, World Changers Church International, the children's ministry is committed to sowing the Word of God in every session. We do this because we understand the importance of imparting wisdom and understanding into each child. We know that one day God is going to use them. Right now He's preparing them. God expects us to do our part in training our children for His purpose. The extent to which you perceive your child's anointing will determine the degree to which you benefit from the gift God has given you.

In 1 Samuel, there is an excellent example of how God used a young child to minister to others. Before Samuel was born, his mother Hannah prayed and believed God for a son. She promised the Lord that if He would give her a son, she would dedicate him back to God and see to it that he fulfilled God's plan and purpose for his life.

1 Samuel 1:11

And she vowed a vow, and said, O Lord of hosts, if thou wilt indeed look on the affliction of thine handmaid, and remember me, and not forget thine handmaid, but wilt give unto thine handmaid a man child, then I will give him unto the Lord all the days of his life, and there shall no razor come upon his head.

Hannah's commitment as a parent did not end there. Every year she and her husband visited the temple to make the yearly sacrifice and to give Samuel the coat she made for him (1 Samuel 2:19). Hannah continued to train Samuel by showing her love for him. She correctly perceived her son as a gift from God and honored his service to the Lord. As a result, Eli the priest blessed her, and she conceived five more children (1 Samuel 2:20,21).

At this time Samuel did not know God's plan for his life. The Bible says he ministered unto the Lord but did not yet know the Lord's voice.

And it came to pass at that time, when Eli was laid down in his place, and his eyes began to wax dim, that he could not see; And ere the lamp of God went out in the temple of the Lord, where the ark of God was, and Samuel was laid down to sleep; That the Lord called Samuel: and he answered, Here am I. And he ran unto Eli, and said, Here am I; for thou calledst me. And he said, I called not; lie down again. And he went and lay down. And the Lord called yet again, Samuel. And Samuel arose and went to Eli, and said, Here am I; for thou didst call me. And he answered, I called not, my son; lie down again. Now Samuel did not yet know the Lord, neither was the word of the Lord yet revealed unto him. And the Lord called Samuel again the third time. And he arose and went to Eli, and said, Here am I; for thou didst call me. And Eli perceived that the Lord had called the child. Therefore Eli said unto Samuel, Go, lie down: and it shall be, if he call thee, that thou shalt say, Speak, Lord; for thy servant heareth. So Samuel went and lay down in his place. And the Lord came, and stood, and called as at other times, Samuel, Samuel. Then Samuel answered, Speak; for thy servant heareth. And the Lord said to Samuel, Behold, I will do a thing in Israel, at which both the ears of every one that heareth it shall tingle. In that day I will perform against Eli all things which I have spoken concerning his house: when I begin, I will also make an end. For I have told him that I will judge his house for ever for the iniquity which he knoweth; because his sons made themselves vile, and he restrained them not.

God spoke to Samuel because Eli would not listen. When God is unable to get the attention of an adult, He will use children for His purpose. In fact, He will use whoever is listening, willing, and available.

Now Samuel needed training because he didn't recognize God's voice. As far as he was concerned, he had heard Eli's voice. That is another reason why we stress the importance of teaching children in our church; they may not yet know the voice of God. Neither do they know how God's plan operates. That's why training is so vital.

God spoke something powerful to Samuel. It is a good thing that he had received training from Eli. Otherwise, the message would have gone over his head and Israel would not have been able to benefit from what he spoke to the nation. Samuel was ultimately obedient to do everything God commanded, but it took some training to get him to that point. Someone had to spend time instilling the Word in him in order for others to benefit from what he heard from the Lord.

God wants to use your children even as He used Samuel. You can take advantage of the opportunity to sow the Word of God into your child's spirit during pregnancy. God depends on you to raise them according to His will and His way.

Psalm 127:1-3

Except the Lord build the house, they labour in vain that build it: except the Lord keep the city, the watchman waketh but in vain. It is vain for you to rise up early, to sit up late, to eat the bread of sorrows: for so he giveth his beloved sheep. Lo, children are an heritage of the Lord: and the fruit of the womb is his reward.

Unless we allow the Lord to teach us how to train our children, love our spouses, and live as families should, we labor in vain. Children are a heritage. They are the assignment God has given to us.

Psalm 127:4 says, *"As arrows are in the hand of a mighty man; so are children of the youth."* Arrows are weapons used against the enemy. That's exactly how God wants to use our children. He wants us to train them so as they get older, they can be used to speak and fight against the devil and his schemes. He wants them trained so they will know how to defend themselves against the devil when he exposes them to drugs, tempts them to follow the crowd, or distracts them from doing homework. God wants them to be able to withstand the attacks of the enemy. Rather than seeing your children as a hindrance to your plans, begin to look at them as a heritage from God.

You have a responsibility to your children above and beyond feeding and clothing them. Here are some of the most important.

1. Teach them the Word of God.

Make sure your children understand God's commands and precepts. Ask God for the wisdom to explain it to them in a way they can understand. The Bible says in Deuteronomy 6:7, *"And thou shalt teach them diligently unto thy children, and shalt talk of them when thou sittest in thine house, and when thou walkest by the way, and when thou liest down, and when thou risest up."* Talk about

God's plans and expectations while you are driving them to school or cooking dinner. Make the study of God's Word enjoyable.

2. Train them to obey God's Word.

In order for your children to obey what is in the Bible, they must see you obeying it first. Children mirror what they see, so be sure your Christianity is a relationship and lifestyle, rather than a label. *"Train up a child in the way he should go: and when he is old, he will not depart from it"* (Proverbs 22:6).

3. Provide for them.

Just as your Heavenly Father gives you what you need for daily living, you, too, should provide your children with what they need for healthy, happy, and productive lives. This principle is made clear in 2 Corinthians 12:14, which says, *"Behold, the third time I am ready to come to you; and I will not be burdensome to you; for I seek not yours, but you: for the children ought not to lay up for the parents, but the parents for the children."*

4. Nurture them.

Your job is to ensure that your children are raised by God's principles, not by the opinions of men. You must allow the Word of God to be the final authority in the parent-child relationship. *"And, ye fathers, provoke not your children to wrath: but bring them up in the nurture and admonition of the Lord"* (Ephesians 6:4).

5. Maintain control of your children.

Control is not a bad thing! In fact, the Bible makes it clear that keeping your children under control is a sign of love. Boundaries must be set and adhered to so that an orderly home can be established. *"One that ruleth well his own house, having his children in subjection with all gravity; (For if a man know not how to rule his own house, how shall he take care of the church of God?)"* (1 Timothy 3:4,5).

6. Love them.

You must love your children and be totally committed to them. Love is not a passing emotion. It is a quality decision. Love always seeks the best for another individual and does what it can to promote their success. ***"But after that the kindness and love of God our Saviour toward man appeared"*** (Titus 3:4).

Child of God, if you don't train and teach your child, someone else will. If you don't handle your responsibility correctly, the devil will take advantage of your lack of interest and use the opportunity for his gain. When you disregard the responsibility God has given you toward your children, Satan will take advantage of your neglect.

When you train your children properly in the things of God, they will not depart from them. They will be so well-trained in God's Word that they wouldn't think of trying to live their lives without Him.

Creflo and I are training our children to apply the Word of God to their lives daily, and not just once a week. They are learning that Christianity is not a label, but a lifestyle.

A REFLECTION OF THE WORD

Traditionally, many pastors have raised children who end up not serving God at all. They were usually children who were rarely taught the significance of living God's way. Serving the Lord was never made practical in their personal lives. Their parents seldom took the time to sit down and explain why things were being done the way they were. As a result, a true commitment to God was never thoroughly established.

Personally, I hated church when I was growing up. Sunday school was boring, the teachers were mean, the chairs were hard, the church was hot, and there was a lot of hollering and screaming. I couldn't wait for church to end so that I could get away from that place. There was little understanding in the teaching of God's Word and how it could be applied to my life. Because of that experience, I've taken time to teach my children so they won't grow up with the same type of church experience. My husband and I both take responsibility for raising our children by teaching them daily through prayer, devotions, and discipline. I want them to know God in a practical way, especially when choosing friends, taking tests, and avoiding temptation. They must understand the importance of angelic protection so they will not be afraid. God doesn't want your child to be unsaved or to get beaten up by the devil. Neither does He want your child to graduate from the school of "hard knocks," just because he or she did not learn the Word or understand how to live.

Our daughter Alex loves domestic things. She loves to sweep, wash dishes, and clean. Our oldest daughter Jordan, on the other hand, has a beautiful voice and can sing very well. We have tried to encourage her to take singing lessons, but she is not interested. We know that God has given her a voice to be used for His purpose. Once we told her that if she didn't want to take singing lessons, we were going to make her take them anyway. That didn't go over so well. However, it encouraged her when we told her that she is anointed to sing and that perhaps God will use her voice to minister someday.

You must be in a position to teach and train your children in the way they should go. There is a difference between teaching and training. To *train* means "to mold one's character or to instruct by exercise." It also means "to drill, make obedient to orders, and point in an exact direction." I like those definitions.

Teaching, on the other hand, involves giving information. There is a time to train and teach your children the importance of learning to pray, read the Word, do chores, and finish homework. As you teach and train, you are pointing them in the direction God would have them to go. You must train your children so well that they know how to obey God and do what He is leading them to do.

There should be no confusion on whether they will follow in Mom and Dad's footsteps or God's. If your lifestyle doesn't mirror the Word, they will be hindered from fulfilling what God has called them to do. When you train them, they must understand that whatever you instruct them to do is neither optional, negotiable, nor up for discussion. They don't have to agree; they just have to obey—that's training.

Don't force them to do optional things like taking voice lessons. If we had made Jordan do that she would have hated it. Eventually she may have adapted, but we did not want to force her to do something she was not required to do. Remember to handle your children with gentleness and sensitivity. Learn how to shape their will without controlling them and breaking their spirits.

DEFINING THE BOUNDARIES

As a parent, you have to define the boundaries and set standards. Discipline shapes the will of a child. It protects and sets guidelines.   Tell your children what is expected and be sure your expectations are age-appropriate. Here are a few ground rules:

1. Your child should know what is and what is not acceptable behavior.

Do not punish your children if they have not been made aware of your guidelines. Make sure they understand the type of behavior you expect from them. Explain what is not acceptable, and let them know that they will be held responsible for their actions.

It is important that they bear the yoke of discipline. *"It is good for a man that he should bear the yoke [of divine disciplinary dealings] in his youth"* (Lamentations 3:27, *AMP*). The discipline you provide is for direction and is a part of overall training. You cannot train your children without correction, reproof, rebuke, and at times, the rod. A child will often test you through disobedience. Nonetheless, effective discipline requires that you use the rod of correction.

2. Respond when your child disobeys.

It is necessary that you respond even when you are tired. There are times when Creflo is resting after returning from a trip or from several sessions of teaching and the kids are at the foot of our bed doing all sorts of things. Although we have already given them instructions not to hit, push, or fight each other, they put us to the test. At that moment, we have the opportunity to respond as responsible parents, or ignore their behavior. If we fail to respond, they will think that it is okay to continue the same behavior over and over again. It is our job to respond appropriately and immediately to disobedience every time.

3. Learn to distinguish the difference between willful disobedience and childish behavior.

You should be able to discern when your children are being rebellious and when they are exhibiting childish behavior suitable to their age. Be careful in your establishment of expectations and be reasonable. Children should never be spanked or disciplined for unreasonable expectations.

4. Teach and reassure your children after they are disciplined.

Hold your children and make sure they understand why they were disciplined and how they can avoid mistakes in the future. This form of nurturing builds love, fidelity, and family unity. Pray with them and ask God to forgive them for their disobedience. Have them ask God for the strength to obey. It is important that your children know that although they have been disciplined for behavior that doesn't line up with the Word, Mom and Dad still love them and will always be there for them. Explain to them that you are directing them in the way they should go.

5. Set reasonable expectations and limits.

It is vital that teenagers, in particular, understand your instructions and are capable of doing what you ask. Often we become frustrated with our children because we assume they are capable of doing what they have been assigned. Seldom do we realize that we have failed to properly demonstrate what should be done.

Make sure you take the time to teach and train them. Don't expect the teen or children's ministry at your church to do all the work for you. Gladly take the responsibility to train your children. Don't allow another person to do it for you.

6. Be guided by love.

According to 1 Corinthians 13:8, love never fails; therefore, be guided by love. It is a guaranteed way to get the best results. Don't allow fear or a threatening disposition to guide you. Rather than fostering unity, fear will create an atmosphere of division. My parents used fear to train and guide me. I was so afraid to disobey that I did exactly as I was told. If I got out of line, I knew Mama would deal with me when we got home. Don't raise your children in such fear that they are in bondage to it. When you allow love to be your guide, they will follow your example when raising their children. They will remember that in your house love prevailed and that the atmosphere was peaceful.

CONCLUSION

Correction, discipline, and love are woven through the fabric of the Bible for Christians in general and therefore should be woven into the lives of our children. *"He that spareth his rod hateth his son: but he that loveth him chasteneth him betimes"* (Proverbs 13:24). According to the Word, if you don't spank your children, you hate them. You may think you are showing them love, but that is not what the Word says. The word *betimes* means "early." Do it while they are young and it will make a great difference as they grow older.

Proverbs 23:13 says, *"Withhold not correction from the child: for if thou beatest him with the rod, he shall not die."* Have you ever spanked your children, and watched them act as if they were dying? I have one of those at home. Before you approach her, she's hollering for dear life. Our children prefer that I spank them because I tend to have a gentler touch. However, my husband tells me that I should not allow them to manipulate me. But you know how mothers are. At times we tend to lean in the direction of our children. I thank God for my husband's leadership and his initiative in seeing to it that we raise our children together. It takes

28

both parents to raise godly children.

Together instruction and correction provide wisdom. *"The rod and reproof give wisdom: but a child left to himself bringeth his mother to shame"* (Proverbs 29:15). When you use the rod, it's as if you are saying, "You are misbehaving because you obviously lack wisdom. Here, let me help you!" A child that does not receive reproof and wisdom is a child that will bring you to shame.

I've seen kids in the grocery store who embarrass their mothers by falling out when they don't get what they want. If one of my children ever did that, I would spank them right on the spot to let them know their actions are not acceptable.

Proverbs 22:15 states, *"Foolishness is bound in the heart of a child; but the rod of correction shall drive it far from him."* When you discipline your children, just remind yourself that you are driving the foolishness out of them. Don't wonder why they do the things they do, because the Bible says that foolishness abounds in them. It also says that the rod will drive it out. It is not your opinion or the opinion of the psychologist that will drive foolishness out of your children. The Word says the rod is the best remedy. We can't allow our children to bring us to shame or to be bound up with foolishness. We must be responsible and remain firm.

Discipline has to occur while your children are young and teachable. That is when there is hope. *"Chasten thy son while there is hope, and let not thy soul spare for his crying"* (Proverbs 19:18). If you wait until your children are grown up and have adopted their own way of doing things, it will be too late. You will not be able to direct them in the way they should go. Discipline early and don't hold back even if they cry. As sweet and adorable as they are, kids quickly learn how to look pitiful. They instinctively know when they are about to be punished. Don't let that stop you from training them up in the way of the Word.

Your ability, willingness, determination, and decision to correct them will bring rest and delight to your soul. *"Correct thy son, and he shall give thee rest; yea, he shall give delight unto thy soul"* (Proverbs 29:17). My husband and I are always blessed when our son Greg comes home. We see the correction and godly instruction we've imparted into him and how he has taken the responsibility, as a man of God, to lead his family. It has truly been a joy to see God's work in his life. If your children don't receive your instruction immediately, continue to pray for them, love them, and stand on the promises of God's Word. Everything God says in His Word will come to pass.

Colossians 3:20–21, *AMP*

Children, obey your parents in everything, for this is pleasing to the Lord. Fathers, do not provoke or irritate or fret your children [do not be hard on them or harass them], lest they become discouraged and sullen and morose and feel inferior and frustrated. [Do not break their spirit.]

The way you choose to deal with your children can either encourage them to fulfill God's purpose for their lives or break their spirits. When their spirit is broken, fear rather than faith, is instilled in them. If that happens, they will not know the difference between what God has called them to do and what you are making them do.

Do not provoke your children to anger. They can easily be provoked to anger and frustration when you are inconsistent. Never discipline in anger, frustration, or resentment. Don't be too hard on them and don't expect too much or you will begin to break their spirit. Instead, operate in the spirit of God's love. Remember to be consistent in your approach to discipline and let the punishment fit the crime.

Teach the principles found in the Word of God. Begin by setting the pattern of consistency in what you do and by getting involved in their activities. Above all, do your best to maintain an atmosphere of prayer and praise.

Follow the Word of God and train your children in the way they should go. God's promise is that when they grow up, they will not depart from your teaching.

How to Train Up a Child *Without* BREAKING His *Spirit*

Taffi L. Dollar

ABOUT THE AUTHOR

Taffi L. Dollar is the wife of Dr. Creflo A. Dollar Jr. Together they pastor World Changers Church International, a non-denominational church of over 20,000 members, located in College Park, Georgia. She is also the Executive Director of World Changers Ministries, the President and CEO of Arrow Records, and the overseer of the Women's Fellowship.

A native of Atlanta, Taffi Dollar obtained a bachelor's degree in Mental Health and Human Services from Georgia State University. She accepted Jesus Christ as her personal Lord and Savior in 1983 while attending a Bible study facilitated by her husband on the campus of West Georgia College. A mother of five, she firmly believes that the best way to raise successful children is by actively demonstrating the divine love and compassion of God found in His Word.

Sister Taffi, as she is affectionately known by her congregation, is an anointed vessel of God. She ministers the gospel of Jesus Christ throughout the country, and can be seen and heard worldwide on the *Changing Your World* radio and television broadcasts.

FIVE STEPS TO COMPLETE SALVATION

1. Recognize and admit that you are a sinner **(Psalm 51:5)**.

2. Repent of your sins **(1 John 1:9)**.

3. Confess Jesus Christ as Lord and Savior **(Romans 10:9,10)**.

   "Father, in the name of Jesus, I recognize and admit that I am a sinner. I repent of my sin and I make a 180° turn away from sin to you by changing my heart, my mind, and direction. I confess with my mouth that Jesus is Lord, and I believe in my heart that you raised Him from the dead. I invite you to come into my life Lord Jesus, and I thank you that I am saved. Amen."

4. Receive baptism by water **(Matthew 3:6)** and the baptism of the Holy Spirit with the evidence of speaking in tongues **(Acts 2:3, 4, 38; Acts 8:14-17)**.

5. Pray, read, and obey the Word of God daily **(1 John 5:3)**.

SEVEN STEPS TO RECEIVING THE BAPTISM OF THE HOLY SPIRIT

1. The Holy Spirit is a gift that was given on the day of Pentecost **(Acts 2:38).**

2. Salvation is the only qualification necessary for receiving the Holy Spirit **(Acts 2:38).**

3. The laying on of hands is scriptural **(Acts 8:17).**

4. You can expect to speak in tongues when hands are laid on you **(Acts 19:6).**

5. Disregard any fears or false teachings about receiving a counterfeit **(Luke 11:11-13).**

6. Open your mouth as an act of faith **(Ephesians 5:18,19).**

7. Receive the gift of speaking in tongues in an atmosphere of peace **(1 Corinthians 14:33).**

BOOKS BY
DR. CREFLO A. DOLLAR JR.

- Answers Awaiting in the Presence of God

- How to Honor Your Man of God

- How to Trouble Your Trouble

- S.O.S. Help! My Flesh Needs Discipline

- The Anointing to Live

- The Color of Love

- The Covenant Connector

- Having Faith for Mysteries

- Jesus Is Our Jubilee

- The Miracle of Debt Release

- How to Get Out of Debt God's Way

- How to Obtain Healing

- El Shaddai: Making a Demand on God's Supply

- How to Train Up a Child Without Breaking His Spirit*

(*) By Taffi L. Dollar

TAPE SERIES BY
DR. CREFLO A. DOLLAR JR.

- The Ministry of the Holy Spirit - Volumes 1 & 2

- The Inheritance of Our Salvation

- Overcoming Impossibilities

- How to Tame Your Thoughts

- How to Overcome the Spirit of Lust:
  An Unquenchable Desire

- Understanding the Will of God - Volumes 1 & 2

- Understanding God's Answer to Racism,
  Separation, and Division

- Making Jubilee a Reality in Your Life

- Having Faith for Mysteries

- Prosperity Profile

- How to Receive the End of Your Faith

- The Miracle of Debt Release

- How to Get Out of Debt God's Way

- It's Time to Believe God

- The Making, Shaping and Molding of Godly Children

- Living Under God's Commanded Blessings*

- Family Matters*

- Kidz Faith Confessions*

(*) By Taffi L. Dollar

JOIN THE TAPE CLUB

By becoming a tape club member, you will receive tapes of each Sunday service monthly by choosing a monthly, quarterly, or annual payment plan.

HEAR the **UNEDITED, UNCUT, AND UNMISTAKABLY CANDID** teachings of Dr. Creflo A. Dollar Jr. as heard by the congregation at the World Dome.

EXPERIENCE the dynamic power and...

SHARE in the excitement, joy, and inspiration as the Word of God is delivered with simplicity and understanding.

IT'S JUST LIKE BEING THERE!!

CREFLO DOLLAR MINISTRIES

PARTNERSHIP HAS ITS PRIVILEGES

Become a Vision Partner

Our part is to:
• Pray daily that God's blessings be upon you.
• Study the Word and diligently seek God on your behalf.
• Minister to you monthly in a personal letter from Dr. Creflo A. Dollar Jr.
• Provide you with an official partner certificate.
• Periodically offer special gifts for your spiritual edification and growth.

Your part is to:
• Pray for us always.
• Be committed to support meetings in your area.
• Support us financially with your monthly pledge (Phil. 4:17).
• Always lift up the ministry, Dr. Dollar, and his family with positive confessions.

If you would like:
• To order books and tapes by Dr. Creflo A. Dollar Jr.
• To become a partner or supporter of Creflo Dollar Ministries
• To obtain a free copy of the *Changing Your World* magazine

Call us:

United States and Canada 866-477-7683

United Kingdom ....+44-121-359-5050

Australia.....................................+61-7-5528-1144

South Africa...............................+27-11-792-5562

Visit our web site: www.worldchangers.org